Proverbs Man

—— *by* ——

Royal Gatson

DEDICATION

To anyone who takes the time to
read this. I appreciate you.

Contents

Acknowledgments

Thank you Alex, for posing a question
that provoked me to write this book.

Thank you Luliana Marin, for
the final edit of the book.

Thank you Rica Cabrex, for the book
cover & formatting the book.

Introduction

While in the office at work, a lot of my coworkers would be there as well. When business slowed down, my coworkers and I would engage in conversation. These conversations varied depending on which coworker I was talking to, but these conversations were bound to be either deep, thought-provoking, or entertaining. This particular day, I can't recall what was happening or what was said prior to my coworker asking me a question that changed my life. She asked, "I know the Bible speaks about a Proverbs 31 woman, but what does the Bible say about a man?"

Initially, I thought about it, but I came to a complete pause because I had no comeback. This is relatively abnormal for me because I am rarely speechless. However, this was a deep question, and I never thought about it before. So, I told my coworker, "I don't know, but I will do some praying and studying and come up with an answer." Side note, it is okay to say "I don't know" sometimes. Don't feel pressured to make up information.

I remember when I asked my father a Bible question once, and he said, "I don't know." It gave me confidence that he would not speak unless he was sure. But I went home and did a little bit of research and came across Ephesians 5 because I have heard others try to make this comparison. Personally, I never thought Ephesians 5 and Proverbs 31 were comparable. While Proverbs 31 seems to be directly referring to women, I didn't feel like Ephesians 5 was directly referring to men only. Instead, Ephesians 5 was written to "dear children" who desired to be "followers of God." Though deep, this scripture applied to all believers and not men only.

Now, I am completely intrigued by the question and must find an answer. Not just for her benefit but for myself as well. As I began to read the book of Proverbs and pray about the topic, God showed me something that I never previously recognized. I knew Solomon wrote a vast majority of Proverbs. I even knew that at times he was recalling what his father, David, told him. When I pieced it all together, I realized Proverbs was written by a king (Solomon) who was instructing his son on how to be a king. Also, it's King Solomon recalling what his father, King David, said to him. In Proverbs 30, Agur, the son of Jakeh, gives profound wisdom also. Even in Proverbs 31:1-9, King Lemuel is recalling the prophecy that his mother spoke to him regarding how a king should conduct himself. The whole book of Proverbs is outlining how a man is supposed to conduct himself if he knows he is a king. This revelation encouraged not only the title of this book but every word within it. The Proverbs Man.

I pray this book will have a lasting impact on both men and women. I believe many men desire to know how to do better. They truly want to know what God expects from us as men. We have heard of the Proverbs 31 woman. However, men want to be equipped with the tools necessary to live this life better as well. My pastor often says, "There is no limit to better." Even if we are doing well as men, the book of Proverbs is laced with profound wisdom that will enable us to do even better. Likewise, my prayer is that many women will be compelled to read this book. Women desire to learn what to look for in a man. Or maybe a single mother is seeking guidance on how to instruct her son in becoming a man. I truly believe that no matter who you are, this book will benefit you.

Now, we are all a work in progress. As I just stated earlier in the introduction, no matter where you are in life, you can do better. Therefore, if you find yourself not possessing every quality of a "proverbs man," that just means improvement can be made. No need to beat yourself up; just find out where you're lacking and make improvements. Solomon wrote the book of Proverbs, but he needed to be corrected by God throughout his life. This wasn't overnight for Solomon, and it may not be overnight for you and me either. While studying and writing this book, I learned several things about myself and realized areas I could improve.

This isn't even a final destination per se, but a journey. A journey to becoming better and better. Though Solomon wrote the book, we realize it was God that gave him the wisdom necessary to write it. Even though the book of Proverbs details out how to be a better man, there is a perfect man who we all should be striving to be more like, and that is Jesus. The goal is to be more and more like Jesus. This is a perfect segue into the first chapter.

1 "What Is His Name, and What Is His Son's Name?"

Proverbs 30:4 "Who hath ascended up into heaven, or descended? Who hath gathered the wind in his fist? Who hath bound the waters in a garment? Who hath established all the ends of the earth? What is his name, and what is his son's name, if thou canst tell?"

The author began this chapter by proclaiming that he was too stupid to even be considered a man. Eventually, we learn the reason the author felt this way was because he didn't know the Holy One on a personal and intimate level. However, the writer did realize there is a God, and that same

God had a Son. At the time of writing this, he may not have known the Son's name.

Nevertheless, the writer knew the Son ascended into heaven and descended to the earth. The Son bound the waters in a garment and established all the ends of the earth. I've come to let you know that the Son's name is Jesus.

Jesus is better!

The introduction places us all on an equal playing field by stating that we are all a work in progress and that we all are working to do better. I've come to proclaim that we all need help from God in order to make this a possibility. The reality is that we cannot do better apart from Jesus. I cringe a little while on social media when I hear about "self-help." Believing you can do better without the help of Jesus is a dangerous and false narrative.

This concept will have you attempting almost anything to reach a level of satisfaction and achievement, only to find that it's fleeting. We definitely need to be active participants in this process, but a helping Hand is needful. On social media, I saw a post that stated, "Get your body, soul, and mind under control and then let God take care of the rest." Well, that doesn't leave too much for Him to take care of, lol.

I know in Psalms 23, David said, "He restoreth my soul." My goal isn't to bash the self-help ideology but to point you to a God that can help you in every aspect of your life and can make you into the man He intended you to be. And I promise this, the man He intends you to be will far surpass who you thought you could be and what you thought you could do. Whatever you envisioned yourself becoming on your own, I promise that God has a plan that is better.

Hebrews 8 declares that our High Priest, being Jesus, is the mediator of a better covenant that is established on better promises. I could break this down and talk about how a covenant is an agreement that differs from a contract because a covenant has no loopholes. A covenant is a partnership between two parties that desire to do everything it takes to make a relationship work. The covenant between two parties can only be broken if one party decides that they no longer want the benefits that the other party has to offer.

Just to clarify, God can't break His covenant with us, or else He lied, and we know that is something He is incapable of doing. We can only break our covenant with Him. The Bible says that Jesus is a mediator of a better covenant and, of course, that is a covenant with the Father. However, I promise that if you put Jesus in the middle of your marriage and family/friend relationships, you will see that those covenants will likewise be better. Matter of fact, put Jesus in the center of any aspect of your life and watch that area of your life get better (but I digressed).

The Bible also says that Jesus helped to establish better promises. If you look at different promises in the bible, you will see that they were intended to make the individual's life better. I am simply saying that Jesus is the foundation and whole embodiment of better. We cannot do better in this life without the help of Jesus.

Saying you cannot do better on your own is not to diminish your abilities or to offend you. The purpose of highlighting this truth is to magnify the significance and the importance of Jesus. When you think about it, that is what humility is; realizing that I cannot do this all on my own and I need some help. We also cannot get the help from the Holy Spirit nor have a relationship with God, the Father, apart from Jesus Christ.

My desire is that you take the time out to read this whole book and grasp every concept within the chapters. Allowing it to transform your life for the better. However, if you don't get anything else from this book, please, grab hold of the fact that Jesus is the key to better. We all need Jesus!

Let us dive into the Bible and learn more about the God who designed us to do better. The first chapter of the book of John starts by saying, "In the beginning was the Word, and the Word was with God, and the Word was God." The next verse continues to say that the Word created everything. We can correlate these scriptures with Genesis 1 that starts by saying, "In the beginning God created the heaven and the earth," and the next few chapters detail out how God created heaven and earth and how He created everything in it.

Therefore, we can conclude that the God who is referred to as the Word in John 1 is the same God of Genesis 1. Allow us to take it a step further. John 1 specifies, "And the Word was made flesh and dwelt among us." If the Word was God and the Word also became flesh, that would mean that the Word could be no one else but Jesus Christ.

The main emphasis of detailing this out was to highlight that Jesus is fully God. But in acknowledging that He created everything, a characteristic of God is then revealed. We see that God is creative. In the beginning, there was absolutely nothing, and with His creativity, He was able to create something out of nothing. Just as I typed that, I got a little excited because I am reminded that He is able.

You may be reading this book and feel that you are so far off from being a "Proverbs Man." I just came to remind you that the same God that saw absolutely nothing and was able to create everything from it is the same God that can meet you where you are and make you into the person you are called to be. He is able. I am pleased to know that no matter how far off I may feel from being the man He has called me to be, the same God that created everything can shape me and mold me into the person I am called to be. He is able!

Because He is creative, we can also be confident in the fact that His will for us is specific and tailor-made just for us. There are some general benefits that will apply to anyone who believes. Such as, He will never leave us nor forsake us and He loves us. Those guarantees are a blessing by themselves, but God still speaks to us individually. What He calls me to do may not be what He called you to do. His creativity gives me the confidence to know that He isn't just calling me to do something just because it worked for someone else. He is calling me to do something that is specific for me because He has equipped me with the skills required to shine in that specific area. I am reminded in Psalms 138 when David said, "The Lord will perfect that which concerneth me…"

Let's jump back into the book of John and notice in verse 4 of chapter 1, it states, "In Him was life, and the life was the light of men." The word for life there in Greek is *zoe*, which would be an active life, blessed life, absolute fullness of life. There is another word for just having breath inside of your body. Family, I'm simply saying that even if you are alive, if you are not in Jesus, then you're not living. We don't want to just be alive. We can be living life in the best way possible and that there is the zoe life.

Growing up, I had a good friend named Nick. We started off as rivals because we were the most athletic kids in the school. In due time, our passion for sports no longer rivaled us against each other but grew us together. As time progressed, we grew closer and closer, and we became brothers. This relationship formed initially through sports, but it branched out over the years on a much deeper level. One of the reasons I believe the relationship flourished instead of faded away is because neither one of us settled or became stagnant in life.

When we were kids, we would say to each other as well as everyone else we encountered, "Are you living life, or are you letting life live you?" We were being humorous, but inside, most jokes ring a touch of seriousness. We didn't realize it at that time, but our comical quote was deep and profound. As kids, everyone is living a similar life, relatively. School, sports, throwing food at lunchtime, you know, just the basics.

But as we grow older, that saying hits a lot harder. As the years begin to accumulate, we see a separation between those who are living life and those who are letting life live them. Brothers, my prayer is that this chapter pushes you closer to the only one that can give you an active, blessed, and full life. That life is found in no one else but Jesus Christ.

And that is good news by itself, but actually, it gets better than that. If we turn to John 10:10, Jesus says, "The thief cometh not, but for to steal, and to kill, and to destroy: I am come that they might have life, and that they might have it more abundantly." Him coming that we would have life is excellent. However, Jesus said He came that we would have life more abundantly. Abundantly meaning superior, something much more, and extraordinary.

Whatever you envision a fruitful, blessed, or active life being, Jesus is able to do more than that. There I go again saying that He is able because I never get tired of reminding myself and others that He is able. I promise He is able to exceed your dreams and make your life better and more abundant. If you stay in Him, then no matter what comes against you (and I promise you that stuff will come against you,) He is able to give you life and life more abundantly. Because He is the God who is able to do exceedingly abundantly above all that we ask or think.

I have heard the term "prosperity gospel," and it is usually viewed in a negative light. I don't know what exactly people mean when they say this phrase or why it usually has a negative connotation. To prosper simply means to do better. The gospel preached and implemented is supposed to make my life better.

I've got to know Him

At the beginning of this chapter, we discovered that the writer of Proverbs 30 declared that he was a stupid man because he didn't know the Holy One in a personal and intimate way. It appears he is being harsh on himself, but in reality, I, likewise, can feel like a stupid man for the same reason. Knowing the Lord has so many dimensions and levels. When walking with the Lord, we will find that some benefits that come with having a relationship with

Jesus are easy to receive. In other areas of our life, it takes more time to believe He is able to help us.

The reason I am struggling in any area of my life is because I don't fully know Him yet. For instance, it may be easy for some to believe He covered my sins, but a little harder for some to believe He can also help me fight addictions. It may be easy to believe that His death on Calvary enabled me to go to heaven when I die. It could be a little more difficult for some to believe that the kingdom of heaven is at hand and He has made some part of heaven available to me right here on the earth. If I ever struggle with believing God is able to do something, that means I haven't fully gotten to know Him yet.

It amazes me that no matter what you know about God, there is always so much more to learn. I have hit points in my life where I believed I knew Him, and then He showed me a different attribute or angle of Himself that I wasn't aware of, and I felt like I was getting to know Him all over again. No matter how deep you are in your walk with God, I promise you can't exhaust Him. I may not get to know Him to His full capacity while here on earth, but I promise that doesn't stop me from trying. It is like a rush of excitement when you learn more and more about Jesus.

Paul actually spoke about this in Philippians 3 when he said, "That I may know him, and the power of his resurrection, and the fellowship of his sufferings, being made conformable until his death." Even within these scriptures, we see different angles of Jesus. We oftentimes just want to know Him in the power of His resurrection, but Paul said I also want to know Him in the fellowship of His sufferings. I want to know Him in all areas and see him from every angle so my relationship with Him can grow and we can get closer and closer.

Usually, what prevents people's relationship with God from growing is their inability to see Him for everything He is. We oftentimes try to put Jesus in a box, and we minimize Him by doing this. When Jesus came to the Earth, the Pharisees didn't know how to view Him. They tried putting Him in a box. When you stop trying to put Him in a box, you will find that He is "I am."

When Moses asked God, "What should I tell the people your name is?" God said, Tell them, 'I am.'" No matter what you need, don't forget the same God who spoke to Moses will speak to you. And whatever you need, He is. If you need a breakthrough, God says, "I am." If you need a miracle, "I am." If you need deliverance, "I am." "I am" is everything that you need!

He is the lamb that was slain before the foundation of the world, but He is also the Lion of the tribe of Judah. He is the God of the hilltops and the God of the valleys. He is the Prince of peace and the Lord of Host. He is the Son of God and the Son of man. He is the king and the servant. He is full of grace but also full of truth. He is everything that we need! We have to stop putting Jesus in a box and see Him for everything He is. He can be both this and that. When we get to know Him more and more, we find that no matter what we are needing or longing for, He is that. Therefore, I want to know Him.

In Psalms 91:14, God said, "Because he hath set his love upon me, therefore will I deliver him: I will set him on high, because he hath known my name. He shall call upon me, and I will answer him: I will be with him in trouble; I will deliver him, and honour him. With long life will I satisfy him, and show him my salvation." We see many promises that God has given David, but these promises are also given to us if we get to know Him like David did.

The scripture states that God Himself will set us on high, not because we are smart, not because we are accomplished, but simply because we know His name and His name is Jesus. Now, there is a difference between knowing His name and knowing what His name is. To know here is the Hebrew word yada. Yada means to learn to know, to know by experience, be acquainted with. All the promises and all the benefits listed in the Bible are contingent on whether or not we know Him. In our journey to get to know Him, we are constantly discovering the greatest gift of all, which is Him. The greatest gift God can give us is Himself. And I want to know everything about Him.

Philippians 2:10-11 "That at the name of Jesus every knee should bow, of things in heaven, and things in earth, and things under the earth; And that every tongue should confess that Jesus Christ is Lord, to the glory of God the Father."

For years when I heard these scriptures, I had a completely wrong view of them. I once thought that at this point, Jesus would force us to get on our knees and worship Him. I turned it into such a violent and aggressive action. However, in this scripture, I don't think we are being forced to get on a knee. I think when we become fully aware of just how supreme and powerful Jesus is, we will not have a choice but to bow down before Him.

It will literally be a natural reaction to the glory of God. One wouldn't even have the ability to refuse to worship Him when we become fully aware of who He is and truly know Him. Just as much as it is a natural reaction to flinch when you believe something is about to hit you, it will be a natural reaction to bow and worship Jesus when we fully know Him. The more we know about Him, the more it makes sense to build our life upon Him. Understanding that building our life upon anything or anyone else but Jesus Christ wouldn't bring about long-term success. Matthew 7:24-27 compares building our life on Jesus Christ and His sayings to building a house on a rock. The rain descended, the floods came, and the wind blew, but because the house was built on a solid foundation, the house remained after the storm.

On the contrary, building our life on anything other than Jesus Christ and His saying is like building our life on a sand foundation. After the storm, the house that was built upon sand was completely destroyed. The qualifications for being a wise man is building your life upon Jesus Christ and His sayings. I want to be a wise man.

2 "For wisdom is better..."

Proverbs 8:11 "For wisdom is better than rubies; and all the things that may be desired are not to be compared to it."

The sentiments expressed in this verse replicate that of proverbs 3. These scriptures combined, we conclude that wisdom is better than silver, better than gold, and better than rubies. As a matter of fact, wisdom is better than anything that you desire and are longing for. We also learn that people with wisdom are blessed. The path will be pleasant and peaceful for those who have wisdom. Wisdom is better.

What is wisdom?

We know that a wise man builds his life upon the Rock being Jesus Christ. What I love about that scripture is that we know nothing more about this man other than he built his life upon Jesus Christ. That alone was enough for him to be considered wise. When we think of someone with wisdom, we tend to think of someone who we deem intellectually advanced. However, wisdom has nothing to do with ACT, IQ, or GPA, though the wisdom God gives can help with all of these things, and I am a living testament of that (I will touch on that later).

My pastor says that wisdom can be simplified to knowing what to do, when to do it, how to do it, where to do it, who to do it with and who not to do it with. Even though this is individualized, so the wisdom God gave me is probably not going to be the wisdom He gives you. What I love about this is we all get put on an equal playing field. If you use the wisdom that God has given you to do what you need to be doing, then no one is wiser than you.

God didn't give them the wisdom to do what He told you to do. He gave it to you. On the flip side, God has given them the wisdom to do something that you probably would not be able to comprehend. If we both apply the wisdom God has given us, that means I am not wiser than you, but you are also not wiser than me. Though the wisdom we receive is different, it is equal. And to God, we are both considered wise men.

An important part in becoming a "proverbs man" is getting wisdom. We see that in the life of Solomon, which, of course, wrote a majority of the proverbs. If you were forced to summarize the ministry of Solomon in one word, it would be wisdom. Solomon was so wise that people came from all nations to listen to his wisdom. However, when Jesus stepped on the scene, He informed the people that the wisdom He has is greater.

Full of Wisdom

We began this book with the same Person we should start everything with, and that is Jesus. One aspect of Jesus that was revealed is, in the beginning, He created everything, and there was nothing made that was not created by Him. Proverbs 3:19 gives us a little more insight on how Jesus was able to create everything. "The Lord by wisdom founded the earth; by understanding hath he established the heavens." We learn that the Lord created the earth by wisdom.

But when you really study the life of Jesus, you will realize that He acted wisely regarding everything He did. I'm in awe by His ability to know when the appropriate time to do certain things is. He perfectly balanced His time and His efforts, and that is something I am trying to replicate as my schedule gets busier and my required tasks increase. He just seemed so fluent in His ability to accomplish all His goals while still finding time to tend to everyone's needs.

He found time to preach to the multitude but also found time to preach to the twelve disciples. Then, at other times, He found the time and knew when it was appropriate to preach to just Peter, James, and John. While on His way to Jairus's house to heal Jairus's daughter, He also thought it was important to stop to talk to the woman with the issue of blood as the Bible stated that she told her whole life story. He went to church regularly because the Bible said it was His custom, but He also found the time to attend a wedding.

I am also in awe by His ability to know exactly what to say to people and knowing exactly how to say it. Because knowing how to say something is just as important as knowing what to say. When we look at the life of Jesus, it is easy to say, "Well, He is God, and He is perfect." This is absolutely true. Jesus is

God, and Jesus is perfect. However, that does not mean that I can't strive to replicate His ways and mannerisms. If my goal is to be more and more like Jesus, I need to stop and see what I can do so I can efficiently and effectively navigate this life like He did.

Eventually, I became aware He was perfect at knowing what to do, how to do it, when to do it, where to do it, and who to do it with because He was full of wisdom. Being full of wisdom is not something that is only applicable to Jesus. We can also be full of wisdom and thus be able to learn how to effectively and efficiently use our time and efforts to navigate this life.

In Luke 2:40, the Bible says that as a child, Jesus was "filled with wisdom." Luke 2:52 says Jesus "increased in wisdom." I don't want to confuse anyone with this, but that would mean as Jesus grew older, He continued to grow in wisdom. Filled with wisdom, to me, insinuates that His wisdom was at maxed capacity. However, just a few verses later to say that He kept increasing in wisdom must mean there are levels to wisdom.

You know the Bible says that we can go from faith to faith. That means from one level of faith to the next level of faith. Mustard seed faith is great initially. But when a mustard seed is planted, it eventually grows into one of the largest trees. Likewise, a small amount of faith is great initially, but eventually, our faith should grow. Likewise, we must be able to go from one level of wisdom to the next level of wisdom. At one point in our life, we may have all the wisdom we need to live a successful life, but then we reach a different level. At this next level, we need more wisdom from God to be able to successfully navigate that level of life.

For instance, I may have the wisdom necessary to do my job, but when I became a supervisor, I needed more wisdom from God to be able to effectively do that job. I may have the wisdom necessary to navigate my life as a single man, but I would need more wisdom to know how to lead a family. Since we go from one level to another, we need more wisdom from God. This keeps us humble because there is always more to learn.

I brought it up, and I realize that it probably raised some eyebrows. How can Jesus, who is God in the flesh, grow in wisdom? Jesus grew in wisdom regarding how to live as an earthly man, and thus He is able to help us when we are being tempted.

Hebrews 2:17-18 "Wherefore in all things it behoved him to be made like unto his brethren, that he might be a merciful and faithful high priest in things pertaining to God, to make reconciliation for the sins of the people. For in that he himself hath suffered being tempted, he is able to succor them that are tempted."

Right there, the Bible says because He was tempted as a regular man, He is able to help us as well. This is how Jesus was able to grow in wisdom. He loved us enough to become like us so He could better understand why we fall short of the mark sometimes, and thus He is able to help us through it.

Think of it this way, Jesus is absolutely perfect and flawless, and everything the Father told Him to do, He did it. He is fully aware that what the Father has planned for our life is way better than anything we can plan for ourselves. The book of Jeremiah would say He is trying to bring us to an expected end. He expects us to be fruitful, multiply, replenish, subdue, and have dominion. This is what He planned for our life at the very beginning. I'm sure He marveled in heaven at our lack of faith and why we would willingly turn from a God who has our best intentions.

When I was twenty-two years old, I got a job as a vocational consultant. The duties of this job included helping individuals either obtain employment or achieve education goals, whether that be a high school diploma, college degree, or certification. When I first started, I primarily worked with clients who had a dual diagnosis. Meaning they had a mental health diagnosis while also suffering from substance abuse addictions.

Like most young individuals starting a career, I came in with a level of zeal and excitement, truly believing I could change the world. Thankfully, I had some success with assisting individuals with getting their lives back on track, but I oftentimes ran into a barrier. This barrier was substance abuse. I thought if these individuals could just quit using these substances, then they would see things change. I remember being frustrated at work concerning this issue, and God said to me, "What do you struggle with that is preventing you from reaching your potential?"

This moment changed the way I viewed my job and honestly changed my life. I have never struggled with substance abuse issues. However, I did have something that I was struggling with and needed to overcome to reach a new level. This enabled me to better understand the shortcomings of the clients I was working with. Now Jesus never struggled with anything, but He was tempted. And because He was tempted as a man, He was able to understand what we are going through more so than when He was in heaven. This is how He grew in wisdom.

Before we talk about the importance of wisdom, or even before discussing what wisdom is, it is necessary to point to Proverbs 9:10, "The fear of the Lord is the beginning of wisdom: and the knowledge of the holy is understanding."

We can't even get to a point where we can begin trying to acquire wisdom until we first have a fear for the Lord. I truly believe before one accepts Jesus Christ as Lord, the only thing you will be hearing from the Lord beforehand is how we need to accept Jesus into our hearts so that we can form that relationship or, as the first chapter explained it, a covenant. I felt it necessary to stop and inform readers of this importance because, without Him, we can't even receive the benefits that wisdom has to offer. We must first have the fear of the Lord.

Now, fear of the Lord is different from the fear most are accustomed to. The type of fear the bible is talking about here has nothing to do with Halloween, the boogeyman, or anything of that nature. Fear here means reverence, honor, or respect. Reverencing, honoring, and respecting God would lead to us submitting our will to His will, obeying Him, and following Him. The reason we know that this is the fear that the verse is referring to is because even the demons are afraid of God. The book of James lets us know that even the demons believe in God and tremble, which insinuates that they are afraid of Him. But of course, we know that the demons aren't getting wisdom from God because if they did, they would have never crucified the Lord of glory. If we fear the Lord or have a reverence, honor, and respect for God, then God will flood our minds with wisdom.

Ask & Seek

Oftentimes, I hear that the Bible is complicated to understand. And I am not trying to be insensitive, but the Bible is fairly simple. It may be difficult to believe some things or difficult to put some things into practice. However, the Bible itself is straight to the point.

Briefly, the benefits of wisdom have been detailed out, but I have yet to say how you can acquire wisdom. It is probably simpler than you would expect. The bible says that if you lack wisdom and want wisdom, then you just need to ask.

James 1:5-8, "If any of you lack wisdom, let him ask of God, that giveth to all men liberally, and upbraideth not; and it shall be given him.

6 But let him ask in faith, nothing wavering. For he that wavereth is like a wave of the sea driven with the wind and tossed.

7 For let not that man think that he shall receive any thing of the Lord.

8 A double minded man is unstable in all his ways."

You would think that acquiring something life-changing like wisdom would require a more complex process. I mean, we just learned that the Lord founded the earth by wisdom. Thank the Lord that He made it simple for a guy like me. I simply need to ask for wisdom. But like I wrote earlier, the Bible is fairly simple and straight to the point. The complex part, at times, is putting it into practice. The dilemma sometimes from me getting everything that God has promised to me is me.

James 1:5-8 says that if we expect to get wisdom from God, then we need to ask for wisdom in faith. Not wavering, not being double-minded but asking in faith. Wavering and double-minded could mean a few things. If I ask God for wisdom but don't expect Him to really give it to me, then I am wavering and double-minded. The verse says if that's how I approach it, then I shouldn't expect anything.

If I ask for wisdom, but I'm not fully committed to applying this wisdom, then I shouldn't expect to receive wisdom. Unfortunately, we have all probably done it before. We ask God for wisdom only to decide whether or not we like what He has to say. Or we ask for wisdom and hope that He cosigns what we already had in our hearts to do. If that is the case, then we should not expect to get wisdom.

We must ask in faith. Saying in our heart and out of our mouth, "Lord, whatever it is that you say, I will do. Whatever you say to me, I believe." If you approach it with this frame of mind, expect God to answer. And expect for God to blow your mind. It has been countless times I have asked for wisdom, and God gave it to me right there. If I was at work, I would say, "Lord, help me to know how to address this situation." If someone has expressed something to me and I can't even find the right words at the moment, I've asked the Lord for wisdom on what to say. Though I expect to receive, He has still blown my mind.

I realized that there were no limits to what God would give me the wisdom to do while I was in college. I was enrolled in an applied statistics course in undergrad. I finished that course with a D, and I struggled to get a D. Math and I did not mix. I then enrolled in grad school, and, of course, one of the courses I was required to take was advanced socio-logical research, which was just advanced applied statistics. This course was built upon the course I took in undergrad. So initially, I was thinking this is going to be a rough semester right here.

But then I really got to thinking about it, and then I said, "If God gave people wisdom to create arks and temples, why can't He give me wisdom in this advanced statistics course?" So, I started praying and asking God to show me how to do these homework assignments. I lie to you not, it would just jump off the page and just start making sense. David said, "The Lord will perfect that which concerneth me." So why would He not help me do some math homework? I often think we limit God by thinking that He only will help us with the churchy things.

Be willing to ask God for wisdom regarding anything.

Ask in faith and expect to receive wisdom and be ready to apply it. Anything less of that would be lacking knowledge and understanding. Lacking knowledge would be not knowing that the Lord is omniscient. If I know He knows everything, then I should never have a dilemma applying the wisdom that He has given to me. Lacking understanding would be not understanding that whatever He says is right and it is better. If I understand that, then I should never have a problem applying the wisdom that He has given to me.

Another important aspect of wisdom is the timeframe we decide to ask for wisdom. Again, the Bible makes this simple for a guy like me. Proverbs 8 prompts us to seek wisdom early. It is important to make asking for wisdom our first response instead of our last resort. I remember I was talking to a friend about something, and I was unsure of what I was going to do. I don't even remember what the issue was, but when I told him about it, he asked one simple question.

"Did you pray about it?" I felt so foolish when he asked that. I would even say I was a little embarrassed. How could I forget to pray about it and ask God for wisdom? Honestly, it can be easy to forget to ask for wisdom early. We start thinking and game planning ourselves and forget to get God involved even though He knows everything. That is why I have come to remind you. I know it is simple, but sometimes life gets chaotic, and we simply need a reminder. Don't make God the last resort but seek Him early.

Surround yourself with wisdom

Wisdom is the foundation of Solomon's ministry. If you really study the relationship between his father, David, and the son Solomon, you will find that

Solomon first learned what wisdom was from his father, David. In Proverbs 4, Solomon is recalling the words of his father, who instructed him to get wisdom. David was a man that did not hesitate to ask God for wisdom in different situations. I am sure David taught Solomon many things, but this seemed to really stick with Solomon. I believe it is because Solomon observed just how crucial it was in David's life.

I recall in 1 Chronicles 14, when David asked God for wisdom regarding whether or not he should go and fight the Philistines, and in verse 10, God said yes, go up. In verse 14, David asked the same thing, but God provided a different answer this time. God said don't go up and fight them but instead go away and circle around them, and when you hear a sound of going, then you should go and fight. What we see right there is David seeking God's wisdom on what to do.

It really highlights the importance of seeking wisdom often because the answer that God provides could be different in different situations. In verse 10, God said go up, but in verse 14, God told David don't go up right now, just wait and circle around them. If David had went and did the same thing without asking God for wisdom, it is possible that the results could have been a lot different this time.

May I suggest to you that no matter what you are encountering, even if you have done it before, you should still ask God for wisdom. God knows all the little details, and if you do the same thing at a different time, you may not have the same results. This keeps us humble as well. Asking God for wisdom forces us to admit that God knows everything, and we do not.

Solomon observed how asking God for wisdom was beneficial for his father, so when Solomon was approached by God, that is what he asked for. In 1 Kings 3 (and 2 Chronicles 1), we see that when God instructed Solomon to ask for something, Solomon asked for wisdom. It is almost like God was testing Solomon to see if Solomon was listening to what his father had been telling him his whole life. Like a final exam with just one question, and Solomon passed. And because Solomon asked for wisdom, God gave him wisdom, but God also provided Solomon with riches, honor, and long life. But Solomon would not have known to ask for wisdom if he was not informed by his father to do so.

This leads me to ask a simple question. Are you paying attention to the examples that you've been given?

Luckily, I grew up as a pastor's son. In my mid-20s, I became a preacher myself. In comparison to others, I had a huge advantage. I had 20 years of accurate biblical teaching to draw from right in my family. If that was placed right before me and I learned nothing, then that is not wise. My parents have been successfully married for over 30 years. If I had that example placed right in front of me and I learned nothing, that is not wisdom.

A wise man looks to draw from people that have been there and done that. A wise man sees what worked for other people and implements these things into his own life. The truth is, no matter what you are striving for, you can always find someone who has done something similar instead of trying to reinvent the wheel and do everything from scratch. Find someone who has accomplished something close to what you seek to accomplish and take notes.

Before getting my master's degree, I asked someone for advice. While buying a home, and even while writing this book, I wanted to learn from others with previous experience. The route to most of my accomplishments was a lot less stressful because I took the time to talk to people before I started. I wanted to know the failures, the successes, the highs, and the lows. I want to know it all, so I can know how to avoid some pitfalls as well as how to achieve some success.

Sometimes, the people you need to draw from are not always directly around you. If that is the case, do your homework to see who you can learn from. But more important than the person's accomplishments, look at the person's character. Draw from people who accomplished their goals the "right way." If someone has acquired prominence, wealth, etc., but all they did was step on people to elevate themselves up, that is not the person to draw from. When a wise man accomplishes something, it shouldn't be at the detriment of others. When a wise man accomplishes something, it should result in himself and others who observe him to say, "Look at what the Lord has done."

Seeking to be surrounded by wise individuals should impact the friends we pick as well. If we understand that wise people exist, we must also recognize that individuals who are not filled with wisdom exist too. The book of Proverbs pulls no punches and labels individuals who don't act wisely as fools. If your circle is full of fools, that probably means it is time to evaluate yourself and determine if you fall in that same category. Fools reject wisdom, instruction, and knowledge. Romans 1 explains what happens when you reject knowledge. Don't be a fool but be a wise man. Having a good group of friends should motivate you, encourage you, and push you to do better. Conversing with folks who lack wisdom is not going to help you to get where you want to be. Nor is it going to help you become who you should be. Surround yourself with wise friends.

When you decide to build your life upon the wisdom of God, others will notice. When others begin to see the benefits of wisdom becoming evident in your life, you will notice a switch in dynamics. You will turn into the person that people desire to learn from because they see the Word working for you. Get wisdom, and watch it change your life.

1 Samuel 18:5, "And David went out whithersoever Saul sent him, and behaved himself wisely: and Saul set him over the men of ware, and he was accepted in the sight of all the people, and also in the sight of Saul's servants."

Acting wisely should cause you to be accepted by all people, no matter the social status. David was accepted by the men of war and servants the same. I like the word yatab in Hebrew, which is the word that is used for accepted. It means to be good, to be pleased, do well, or do right. I am not sure the text necessarily means everyone is jumping up for joy that David was put in charge. That may have been the case for some people, but I doubt that's the case for all.

I'm sure that some people felt they could have led the troops if given the opportunity. However, everyone at least realized that putting David in charge was the right thing to do, and they were confident that he was the right man for the job. This would not have been the reality if David did not conduct himself wisely. But because David conducted himself wisely, he received a leadership role within his workplace. Likewise, act wisely and watch yourself get promoted amongst your peers as well. The benefits of wisdom are endless.

3 "Whatsoever thy hand findeth to do, do it with thy might..."

Ecclesiastes 9:10 "Whatsoever thy hand findeth to do, do it with thy might; for there is no work, nor device, nor knowledge, nor wisdom, in the grave, whither thou goest."

Normally for the titles, I have been using verses from the book of Proverbs. However, Solomon also wrote the book of Ecclesiastes. In the book of Ecclesiastes, Solomon is searching to find the meaning of life. In the earlier chapters, he is quite confused about what really matters in life; everything seems like vanity and meaningless. But during the later chapters of the book, he began to realize and recall the reason for his existence.

In Ecclesiastes 9:10, Solomon tells the audience to do everything to the best of their abilities now because everyone must move on from this life eventually. Mentioning this truth is not to discourage the reader but just the opposite. It is mentioned to encourage the reader to take advantage of opportunities while you have the chance. Utilize your talents and apply yourself now. Solomon highlights that there is no work, device/planning, knowledge, nor wisdom in the grave, which means we should work, plan, use wisdom and knowledge now while we are on the earth.

Though at first glance work, planning, knowledge, and wisdom appear to be independent of each other, they all work hand in hand. Work is the finished product when the rest of the three steps have been achieved. Meaningful work can come about when a goal has been strategically planned. If you are working but have no plan, then you are not successfully working but spinning your wheels. How can you strategically plan if you don't have knowledge of what it is you want to do? If you ever tried to plan without fully knowing what you wanted to do, then you know it's an exhausting journey that leads you nowhere. Lastly, I know what I'm supposed to be working towards by seeking wisdom and acting wisely in whatever position I'm currently in. Solomon tells us to put all the four together and accomplish what you desire to accomplish on this earth. As long as breath is still in your body, you should be working towards something.

I have heard it said that most people give up on their dreams somewhere in their mid-twenties. I can't speak for every country, but here in America, that is usually when people finish post-high school education of some sort. Once the job is obtained, and the house is bought, the wife is married, and the kids are begotten, we usually figure we've "made it." From that point, it seems like a good place to settle, and people either stop dreaming all together or dreams are put on the backburner. Now, when you have a family and other obligations, sometimes dreams need to be put on the backburner for the betterment of the family. If a goal you're reaching for requires you to fall away from your family, then it is not good, and it is not God. But when you feel led by the Holy Spirit, that insinuates the time is right. When the time is right, don't let complacency cause you to be disobedient.

The word "calling" is thrown around often, especially among Christians. Some people search their whole life trying to figure out what they are called to do. I think people are waiting to be stopped in their tracks and for God to speak to them audibly while He shines a light from heaven like He did to Saul/Paul. I will admit, if that happened, then knowing our calling in life would be very easy to recognize. But that did not happen to me. Nor did that happen to anyone that I know personally. I would never say it couldn't happen; God can do anything He wants. However, I am not sure that this is the primary way we find what we are called to do.

So, if God doesn't shine a light from heaven and speak to us audibly, how can we know what we are called to do? By doing everything you do to the best of your abilities. But in order to do everything to the best of your abilities, that innately means you have to be doing something. Doing nothing and waiting for God to tell you something about the course of your life is usually not the answer. God can speak to whoever He wants, however He wants. However, as I began to study, I noticed a trend. When Jesus called the disciples to follow Him, they were usually right in the middle of working.

Mark 1:16-20, "Now as he walked by the sea of Galilee, he saw Simon and Andrew his brother casting a net into the sea: for they were fishers.

17 And Jesus said unto them, Come ye after me, and I will make you to become fishers of men.

18 And straightway they forsook their nets, and followed him.

19 And when he had gone a little farther thence, he saw James the son of Zebedee, and John his brother, who also were in the ship mending their nets.

20 And straightway he called them: and they left their father Zebedee in the ship with the hired servants, and went after him."

When Jesus called Simon Peter, Andrew, James, and John, they were all currently fishing. This was not an activity they were doing in their leisure time. Fishing was the occupation for these four disciples. Likewise, in Mark 2:14, when Jesus called Matthew, the Bible says he was working at the tax collector booth because he was a tax collector. When Jesus called Phillip to be a disciple, many believe Philip was currently a disciple of John the Baptist. Aside from Philip bringing Nathanael to Jesus, nowhere else in the scriptures does the Bible explain how the other disciples were called.

It makes me ask, why did the Bible make an emphasis on showing that the disciples who were called by Jesus were currently working? What did Jesus see in these men that caused Him to tell these disciples "follow me?" Maybe it was work ethic, consistency, dedication, and perseverance. Jesus healed beggars, but oddly enough, that was not the individuals He chose to find and proclaim "follow me" to. In one place in the Bible, Jesus cast out unclean spirits out of a man and told him to go back home and tell them the great things the Lord has done. In most situations, that sounds like a natural sequence of events. However, Jesus said this after the man proceeded to follow Jesus into the boat. Jesus didn't do this to be mean to this man or to demean him. But it does further clarify just how important doing something to the best of your abilities is to Jesus. At that moment, it appears He didn't see it fit to have someone follow Him who wasn't used to working.

I often hear people say they are quitting certain jobs or tasks because they don't believe it will get them where they desire to be. But I'm not sure how they came to this conclusion. Especially when the person who is saying this usually is unsure of where they desire to be. I'm sure Peter never imagined another day in the office would lead to him becoming an apostle. I am sure that David never thought that tending to the sheep was preparing him to win a war for his country.

Do you despise the current role or position you are in right now? Truthfully, the only reason you may feel like this is because you have a hard time believing God is doing something during this season. Stay faithful in whatever role or position you are currently in. Even when it looks like nothing is happening, God is doing something. This is preparing you for the next phase of life.

From personal experience, I have found that nothing I did was wasted. Several times I have prepared for a message and been studying scripture for hours or even days. Then a couple of days before it was time to preach, I would feel the Spirit pushing my message in a different direction. Occasionally, I don't end up using any of the scripture I took all that time to study in the message. Initially, it may feel like I just wasted my time studying the text if I wasn't even going to use it. But then, out of nowhere, the scripture I spent time studying becomes relevant either in a flow of conversation or in another message. I may not recognize the relevance of the text I was studying until years later. But eventually, I will use it. Nothing is ever wasted.

You may be in college and taking a class and wondering what is the point? You may be working a job that you deem as a dead-end job. Just continue, do it with all your might, and eventually, you will see that this was not in vain. Where will it lead you?

I have no idea. However, I am confident that God will use it.

In 1 Kings 19, God told Elijah to return to Damascus. When he got there, Elijah was told to anoint the prophet that would be replacing him. This prophet would end up being Elisha. When Elijah met Elisha, he threw his cloak or robe on him. This demonstrated that Elisha had just been anointed. But when they met, Elisha was plowing the land with twelve oxen. How was plowing with twelve oxen going to prepare Elisha in his new role as a prophet? I don't really have the answer to that question, but it did. You never know how God will use your current situation to prepare you for your future. Just be confident that He will use whatever current role you are in to prepare you.

What should I do?

The importance of doing something has been highlighted. That may force some to say, what should I do? My answer is, do what you can. Particularly when it comes to ministry, if you feel like something is lacking, then that is probably what you need to be doing. If you are in church and the video production quality thoroughly bothers you, that probably is what you need to be doing eventually. For me, I noticed that if I heard someone explain the scriptures inaccurately, that would really bother me. To a point that I couldn't even sleep all night, it was that bad. If you ever feel like something is missing or lacking, that is probably what you need to be doing.

Coincidently, that was the position that Luke was in. When reading Luke 1, the writer is primarily talking about the birth of Jesus and John the Baptist. Both Jesus and John the Baptist were prophesied about several years before they were both physically born. However, though the chapter is primarily about Jesus and John, notice that Luke slyly explained to us how he got into his ministry in the first few verses.

Luke 1:1, "Many people have set out to write accounts about the events that have been fulfilled among us. 2 They used the eyewitness reports circulating among us from the early disciples.[a] 3 Having carefully investigated everything from the beginning, I also have decided to write an accurate account for you, most honorable Theophilus, 4 so you can be certain of the truth of everything you were taught."

Simply put, Luke saw others writing a book about the life of Jesus based on learning from those who witnessed his teachings and miracles firsthand. Luke himself did his research to learn about the accurate account of Jesus. Therefore, he wrote a book so that others could have the same information. At the time, there is no way Luke knew that thousands of years later, we would be reading his books. He saw a need and used his talents to fulfill this need.

If you're unsure of what you need to be doing, you should ask yourself—What needs to be done? I have heard it said that "necessity is the mother of invention." In my last few semesters of college, the term social entrepreneur was used often. A social entrepreneur is someone who starts a project or business with the goal of sparking social change or addressing social problems. I remember being inspired by people who changed cities and even countries by addressing an issue they found in society. Sometimes we can stress ourselves out trying to figure out what we should be doing when the answer might be right in front of our face.

Use what you have

I have been on social media and seen the question posed, "What would you do if you had a million dollars?" Then different people comment on the status and say what they would do if they had that type of money in their bank account. The ideas are grand and intriguing. Such as investing in real estate, stocks, forming LLC, and helping others who need it. However, a lot of the things they would do if they had a million dollars, you don't need a million dollars to do it.

Honestly, if I had a million dollars in the bank, it wouldn't change much for me. I'm already a giver, I already invest in stocks, I already invest in real estate, and I already save money. The level at which I do these things would be magnified, but it wouldn't be a new concept. What makes someone think if they had more money, they would all of a sudden change their habits? Are you using the extra $150 you have monthly wisely? Instead of daydreaming about what you would do if you had something, start where you are and use what you have.

We mentioned John the Baptist briefly earlier. John understood that his calling was to prepare the way for the Lord. Therefore, he declared to the people to repent because the kingdom of heaven was at hand. Repenting is turning away from anything that is drawing you away from God and to look to Him. Also, he baptized the people who would be an outward display to everyone that they have been changed inwardly. In the first chapter of the book of John, the Bible specified that John the Baptist was baptizing others in Bethabara, which was near

Jordan. A couple of chapters later, we learn that John actually began baptizing in another location

John 3:23, "And John also was baptizing in Aenon near to Salim, because there was much water there: and they came, and were baptized."

While first reading, I remember inquiring as to why John switched locations. Then I realized the answer. The reason he switched locations is because there was much water there. That may sound simple, but that is precisely the point. John needed to baptize, so he used a body of water that he found. Use what you have.

Remember when Moses doubted that the people would listen to him in Exodus 4? The Lord asked Moses, "What is that in thine hand?" Moses had a rod in his hand, and that same rod would be used to turn the Nile blood-red and to part the Red Sea. When God was working through Elisha to help the widow woman in 2 Kings 4. the prophet asked the woman, "What hast thou in the house?" The woman only had a pot of oil, but God did a miracle there so the oil would be multiplied exponentially. If God has called you to do something, He will give you everything you need to accomplish it. If you didn't get anything new, that must mean you have everything you need. Use what you have.

An important part of becoming the man we need to be (and a man worth marrying, I might add) is working. When God created us, He designed us to be individuals that worked. In the book of Genesis, after God got done working, He then said, "Let us make man in our image." God designed us to emulate Him. One thing God did six out of the seven days was work. Likewise, we should be working individuals and seeking to accomplish everything we can while we are on this earth. Six of the seven days God worked. However, He did take one day to rest. Since we are made in His image, we likewise should take time after work to rest.

4 "My son, eat thou honey, because it is good..."

Proverbs 24:13 "My son, eat thou honey, because it is good; and the honeycomb, which is sweet to thy taste:"

When reading this verse, at first glance, it seemed a little misplaced. I know the book of Proverbs often feels like a collection of individual thoughts. But at the beginning of the chapter, Solomon is telling his son to get wisdom, avoid people who are plotting evil, take the time to help others, etc. Then, seemingly out of nowhere, he tells his son, "Eat honey because it's good." I know in verse 14, he continues on to compare honey to wisdom, but it still feels random or capricious. It is almost like Solomon is getting hungry in the middle of a task and recalling how delicious honey is. It also appears Solomon is putting just as much emphasis on eating honey as he does the proverbs that preceded this verse.

So, I stopped, and I started reading this text in different translations to see if it would make more sense. (Side note, I once had to explain this to someone who felt less of a Christian because they struggled with understanding the King James Version of the Bible. It is okay to read other versions). I then began to study the text in the native language to determine what honey represents. Naturally, my mind wandered to entering the Promised Land, which was flowing with milk and honey to see if the two texts would work in conjunction with each other. Eventually, I saw some correlation between the text, but a revelation occurred, and I realized the significance of the verse.

Contrary to what it may seem, Solomon didn't get hungry suddenly when he told his son to eat honey. Notice, right before that verse, he was telling his son different proverbs, and then he paused and said, eat honey, it's good. Solomon was informing his son that in the middle of taking care of different tasks, you got to find time to enjoy the things life has to offer because they are good. Solomon didn't say, son, if you want, and if you have time outside of your busy schedule, you should taste the honey. Solomon was instructing his son to make time to enjoy the honey. Take the time to acknowledge the good. Take the time to appreciate the little things.

In the book of Genesis, when the creation is being detailed out after God created everything, He then paused and acknowledged that what he had done was good. Then He went on to the next mission, and then after He did this, He recognized it was good again until He created everything. I love how God leads by example in everything that He does. Even God took time to pause in between different duties and acknowledge the good. Likewise, we should be doing the same thing.

In Philippians 4:8, Paul said, "Finally, brethren, whatsoever things are true, whatsoever things are honest, whatsoever things are just, whatsoever things are pure, whatsoever things are lovely, whatsoever things are of good report; if there be any virtue, and if there be any praise, think on these things." Paul said, whatever is good, you need to think on these things. When you stop and appreciate the things life has to offer that are good, it should cause you to recall that God created all of this.

When you recall that God created this, you are then reminded of the fact that everything that God created is good. When you go through Genesis again, you will recognize that God created everything, and then He created man, then women, and again professed that it was good. Sequentially, it should be highlighted that God created everything before He created humans.

Why is this so? It is not because it was the last creation on God's mind, but, on the contrary, it was the first thing on God's mind. Pastor Jerry Gatson often says God created the light because He knew I could not see without it. God doesn't need the light; everything is naked and opened unto His eyes. God created water and the fish and the fruit because He knew that I not only need this to survive but also because He knew I enjoy it. God created all these good things for me. That is why He created humans last because He created all things on this earth for our good.

When you take time to eat the honey, you recall the fact that it is good because it was made by God. I am in awe when I perceive the attention to detail God has. Notice how God put honey on the earth simply for me to enjoy. Simply because He knew that I would enjoy the taste. It's the acknowledgment of the little things God has done for me that I often overlook that make me realize how good He is to me and just how much God loves me.

In the book of Exodus, the children of Israel were promised by God that they would enter a land that was flowing with milk and honey. However, that did not prevent the people from enjoying the honey they currently had. If you recall, in the book of Exodus, the Lord was sending down manna from heaven. This manna was described as a wafer that is covered with honey. Right here, we see that they are not yet in a place that has a copious amount of honey, but they are still able to enjoy honey daily because the Lord provided it.

How often do we believe that we will feel a sense of fulfillment when we get "there?" "There" is different for everyone. For some people, it is when I get my degree, my car, my house, that job, my spouse. I cannot tell you how many times I impatiently waited to get "there," not appreciating the current situation I was in. I know I am not alone on that because I have seen other people do the same thing.

We tend to think the next stage of life will bring a sense of fulfillment. And Hallelujah, it will bring fulfillment, but that should not prevent us from stopping and enjoying the honey that we currently have right in front of our face. It will be difficult to make it to the next phase of life if you don't take the time to enjoy your current situation. It will feel like a constant fight to get to this destination, and it will often feel so far away.

And because it feels far away, it will be difficult to continue with the daily grind because you think it will never lead you to the desired destination. This way of thinking had caused many people to quit right before they reached their goal. This can be avoided if you take the time to stop and enjoy the honey. Take the time to recognize the good in your current situation, no matter where you are.

Even if you are in a valley, take the time to enjoy your current situation. I am telling you from experience, the valley has many benefits. Take Elijah for an example; God called Elijah to go to the book of Cherith in isolation. Isolation at the time can feel like a boring, pointless season of life. However, there is plenty of good that can be found at this time.

Now, the Bible doesn't directly say Elijah was in isolation, getting closer to God, but we can infer this based on comparing his valley to that of John the Baptist. Also, I am confident this was the case because as soon as Elijah left the valley, God called him on different missions, and his ministry from that moment forward was nonstop. He would not have had the faith to do what God had called him to do if he wasn't getting closer to God in the valley.

After leaving the valley, God called him to raise children from the dead, battle false prophets, and many other things. Now, this seems like a blessing, and it is, but this can also be a stressful thing. It seemed like Elijah no longer had downtime. Eventually, Elijah ends up running away and hiding in isolation. If you are alone in this season, look for the good that comes from it because when God calls you out of that season, you will find that downtime becomes a little harder to come across.

Not to veer left, but if you are single in this season, enjoy the honey (no, I didn't say honeys). There are plenty of benefits to singleness. Right now, in my stage of life, I can pretty much move however I would like. I don't have to consider anyone else's schedule, and this is good. I've been able to study the Bible for hours at a time without any interruptions, and this too is good.

I often say I want to be married and have kids in the future, but I realize that the duties of a father and husband never cease. It is hard work. It is definitely worth it, and I wouldn't doubt that these would be the absolute best times of my life. However, I am still aware of the fact that it will be the hardest work of my life. So, I enjoy the singleness while I have it.

You can find the honey in any situation if you look for it. Sometimes we are waiting until we enter the land that is flowing with milk and honey, but we need to stop and enjoy the honey right now.

God promised to lead the children of Israel into the Promised Land, which was flowing with milk and honey. We assume that enjoying the honey becomes natural when honey seems like it is more prevalent, but that is not necessarily true. Most people would still find themselves anxious during this time. "How long will this honey be here?" "How long will we be in this land?" "Should I start looking for a new land now just in case this falls through?" Someone read this and laughed because they knew it was true. Learning to enjoy the honey is a skill that takes time to develop. Learn to cultivate this skill. God can send you to a land flowing with milk and honey, but this does you no good unless you take the time to enjoy it.

The benefits of singleness were just highlighted, but I also want to discuss the opposite side of the spectrum. While reading this and correlating it with other verses, I believe Solomon is also informing his son about marriage. I will list a couple of verses and then make my point.

Song of Solomon 4:11, "Your lips drop sweetness as the honeycomb, my bride; milk and honey are under your tongue. The fragrance of your garments is like the fragrance of Lebanon."

Ecclesiastes 9:9, "Live joyfully with the wife whom thou lovest all the days of the life of thy vanity, which he hath given thee under the sun, all the days of thy vanity: for that is thy portion in this life, and in thy labour which thou takest under the sun."

If we link these two scriptures, as well as the scripture I started the chapter with, we notice that Solomon is actually telling his son something very profound. In one verse, he tells his son to enjoy the honey because it's good. In Song of Songs, which is also written by Solomon, he compares the lips of his bride to honey. In the last verse, Solomon is realizing that his portion or reward in life is enjoying his life with his wife. I believe Solomon is informing his son that when you are married, make sure to enjoy time with your wife.

This may sound obvious, but I am going to remind you that Solomon is the king of Israel. Being that Solomon is the king, I am sure that there are a million places he could be and a million things he could be doing. As responsibilities pick up, tasks and duties also pick up. However, Solomon informs us that you must make time for your spouse. His word choice didn't give the vibe that this was an optional recommendation either. However, this is just as mandatory, if not more important, than all the other duties. Enjoy your honey now.

5 "And why wilt thou, my son, be ravished with a strange woman...?"

Proverbs 5:20 "And why wilt thou, my son, be ravished with a strange woman, and embrace the bosom of a stranger?"

The words of wisdom that lead up to this verse, Solomon is informing his son of the consequences that will occur from dealing with strange women. We are also forewarned that her feet lead you to death. Relationships with the strange woman will cost you honor, strength, and even your hard-earned wealth will find itself in the house of this woman. This relationship will even have the potential to bring you to complete ruins in front of everybody. So, in verse 20, Solomon stops and asks his son, why would you do it? How will dealing with strange women lead to this much destruction?

When the Bible says this can cost you your strength, I will first use an example of a married man. If a man is married yet is also dealing with strange women, he will find himself trying to live two separate lives. You have to be home but also find time to step out to entertain that situation. Obviously, you have other duties that need to be fulfilled as well. Consequently, something has to drop off because you are making time for someone you should not be making time for. Now your strength is divided, and you are stretching yourself thin and exhausting yourself trying to find time for everything, but you can't. Because the individual's priorities are messed up, they will likewise see it impact their schedule and efficiency. This doesn't just apply to married men either.

As a single man, if you are having sex before marriage, you will often feel that your strength is divided. Even if she is not a "strange woman," which is usually in reference to a woman who is committing adultery. Even if she is your girlfriend, you will find that your strength is divided, and it becomes difficult to juggle all of your duties. You think it is the relationship that is tying you down and thus preventing you from reaching your goals. It is actually the premarital sex, I promise you.

The Bible also says that dealing with the strange woman will cause your hard-earned money to be in her house. This can happen in various ways. In some cases, they need to pay the woman so that she doesn't expose this secret to everybody. In other cases, people will take their money to pay to have sex with women. This may sound vulgar, but when people don't have their flesh under control, you will be surprised at what lengths people will go to satisfy their flesh. If this continues, it will eventually blow up in your face and then become public knowledge to everyone. We have seen this happen to many leaders before. That is why I believe, most importantly, that before addressing the strange woman, I need to stop and address my deficiencies. There will always be strange women in the world. However, if I get myself under control, the strange women don't have to be something that causes my life to spiral downward.

Let's address the strange man

As you read through the book of proverbs, you have probably seen strange woman used multiple times.

However, to my knowledge, the term strange man is never used. Some people have questions regarding this, and it is necessary to address it. As we know, the book of proverbs, for the most part, is a book written to a son. I believe the writer never mentioned strange men to his son in a sexual context because that was not something that would have crossed the writer's mind.

That being said, if Proverbs was a book written by a queen to her daughter, I have no doubt in my mind that strange men would have been addressed and viewed in the same light as strange women. I found it necessary to speak on this because I don't want you to think it can only be a woman keeping a man from getting closer to God. This can go both ways. Before I begin to even address the strange woman, I think it is necessary as a man to first examine myself. Before I can even speak on avoiding the strange woman, I have to see what inside of me needs to be addressed. Why am I attracted to the strange woman? Those are questions that need to be addressed first. Prior to examining external factors, I first need to examine the root of the issue, and I need not to look any further than myself.

James 1:14-15 states, "But every man is tempted, when he is drawn away of his own lust, and enticed. Then when lust hath conceived, it bringeth forth sin: and sin, when it is finished, bringeth forth death."

The book of James tells us that the only thing that can cause us to be tempted is something we are lusting after. If I am not lusting after it, then there is no way it can tempt me. Thus, it cannot draw me away from God. For instance, everyone has different things that they have lusted after at one point in their life or another. However, for me, cigarettes were never one of them. You can put as many cigarettes in my face as you want, but that will not cause me to want to smoke.

It isn't something I lust after. But I do have things I've lusted after, and I have to address this issue within me to find out why I'm lusting after them. It is necessary to locate the root cause of the issue, and that is the lust within me. That way, I am not blaming my own personal lust issues on the strange woman. It is easy to blame Delilah for the downfall of Samson, but if you go back and read the story in the book of Judges, this was Samson's fault. Samson had time and time again to leave this situation, but he chose not to do so.

I believe if we find ourselves in similar situations, God gives us multiple chances to walk away before the situation leads to complete destruction. We have to choose to ignore the signs and choose to stay. At that point, the stronghold is so powerful that we fail to make logical decisions anymore. That is why it is so important to examine ourselves so we don't find ourselves in this situation. If you find yourself doing something you shouldn't be doing, the Holy Spirit will let you know it is not right. If we choose to ignore the voice of the Holy Spirit, the voice eventually gets dimmer and dimmer. If this continues, it can be hard to hear the voice of God at all.

1 Thessalonians 5:19 informs readers to not quench or extinguish the Spirit.

The Spirit is here to give us wisdom and to point us to the truth. The Spirit gives us the ability to love, have joy, peace, patience, kindness, goodness, faithfulness, gentleness, and self-control. Therefore, we don't want to extinguish the Spirit by ignoring the Spirit. The reality is, if you ignore God in one area, it becomes easier to ignore God in other areas. If this accumulates, it is possible to find yourself not listening to anything God has to say. That is why it is important to listen to the Spirit when He speaks and to get ourselves under control. That way, the strange woman doesn't have to be something we struggle with for the rest of our lives.

Avoiding the strange woman

What exactly does the Bible mean when it says strange woman? The word strange here is defined as foreigner or alien. Now, I am forced to park right here for just a minute. This is in no way, shape, or form discouraging people from marrying individuals from different nations or different races. I know in Deuteronomy, it states that the people of Israel should not intermarry with the seven nations. That wasn't due to race, but because at this time, these nations didn't believe in the only true and sovereign God. I am ashamed that I even felt the need to explain that. Unfortunately, I have heard church-going folks say they didn't believe in interracial marriage. Even in 2020, that is something that some church-going folks believe (notice, I'm reluctant to say Christians). God in no way, shape, or form would say marrying outside of your race is a sin. Just to clarify.

Anyhow, a strange woman is usually explained in three different ways in the Bible. A woman who doesn't have a relationship with God. A woman who forgets the covenant of her God. An adulterous woman who cheats on her husband. The Bible doesn't speak against marrying outside of race, but it does speak against marrying outside of the faith.

Amos 3:3 "Can two walk together, except they be agreed?"

The reason for this scripture is fairly simple; one person is bound to change the other. I can't speak for everyone; I can only speak on what I have personally seen. When a believer ends up dating someone who didn't believe, it's usually the believer who would be changed. The reality is that every relationship requires compromise at times for the relationship to work. However, my personal relationship with God is not something I can afford to waver on. I don't know when you will read this, but I am currently writing this chapter in 2020 when a global pandemic altered life around the world.

Coronavirus has negatively impacted numerous amounts of people physically, financially, emotionally, and mentally. However, times like this highlight why it is so important to be with someone who believes God is able because I can't/won't let coronavirus cause me to slip spiritually. It is important that my spouse believes in the same God who can still open doors, who can still make a way, and who can still protect and heal my body. Even during a pandemic. That is why the Bible discourages us from marrying anyone who is outside of the faith. It is not to "hinder us from having fun" or anything of that nature, but it is to protect us.

Whenever the book of Proverbs speaks on the strange woman, it almost always starts by emphasizing the importance of keeping wisdom, laws, and commandments. Wisdom, laws, and commandants would, of course, represent the word of God. Which would lead me to believe that getting involved with a strange woman would cause me to fall away from the word of God.

An adulteress woman who is willing to cheat on her husband is also considered a strange woman in the book of proverbs. I know it sounds like common sense, but nothing good comes out of sleeping with another man's wife. I don't care if they are separate or if they say their relationship is open; there is absolutely no benefit. At that moment, the temporary thrill may seem worth it, but in the end, it will only lead to destruction.

I remember I was talking to someone about this, and I posed a simple question. Where do you think that will lead you? Eventually, the husband will find out. When he does, I doubt he will be okay with it. In reference to a husband finding out, the Bible says this.

Proverbs 6:34, "For jealousy is the rage of a man: therefore, he will not spare in the day of vengeance."

Translation, this transgression could lead to an all-out war. Let's say, for some reason, it didn't lead to an all-out war between the men, and you end up with the woman. Can trust really be developed? I don't have the answer to that question. However, I will also never take the time to find out that answer myself. Do yourself a favor. Avoid the woman that is already married. Nothing good will come from it.

What does the Bible say about Porn?

Being that the Bible was written thousands of years ago and they didn't have advanced technology like we currently do, some people think the Bible doesn't answer the question on pornography. No matter the era, you can always open up the Bible and find something that relates to what you are currently going through right now. This topic is no different.

Psalms 119:37, "Turn away mine eyes from beholding vanity; and quicken thou me in thy way."

Vanity means emptiness or worthlessness. The writer informs the audience that if it isn't beneficial to look at, then stop looking at it. Porn would fall into the category of worthlessness, so this scripture would apply.

In the New Testament, if you look at the word fornication in the native Greek language, it is the word *porneia*. Which means illicit sexual intercourse, adultery, and metaphorically stands for the worship of idols. The Greek word *porneia* is, of course, where the English word porn came from. It is crazy that something could be so blunt and blatant. Don't fall victim to this bad habit. It may seem harmless, but it is the very opposite.

It is not informative. You are not learning helpful information that you can implement when it is time for the real thing. Instead, you're extinguishing the Spirit and hurting yourself. For some people, they may even begin to behold things that aren't even natural and find themselves intrigued. Never forget, what is done in the dark repetitively will be brought to the light eventually. You can end up doing things you never thought you would do.

Then you will look up and say, "How did I get here?" You don't just wake up one day as a sex addict or doing things sexually you never thought you would do. It is gradual. It may just begin from you watching it occasionally. It probably won't stay as something you watch only. It will eventually become something you are doing. Avoid it; keep your eyes from watching it because it will not benefit you in any way.

Two-edged Sword

Proverbs 5:3-5

"3 For the lips of a strange woman drop as an honeycomb, and her mouth is smoother than oil: 4 But her end is bitter as wormwood, sharp as a two-edged sword. 5 Her feet go down to death; her steps take hold on hell."

The Bible compares a strange woman to a two-edged sword. Now, we know from the book of Hebrews that a two-edged sword divides the soul and spirit. If a person gets entangled with a strange woman, then it serves as a division between the soul and spirit. During this division, the spirit is being cut out, so therefore, the person is following the soul. If the spirit of man is diminished, it means that the individuals' relationship with God is being cut out. The person may not realize it because it is happening gradually. If this continues, the person is getting farther and farther from God.

When you get farther from God, it gets harder to hear from God. Honestly, at that point, hearing from God not only gets harder, but if this progresses, it probably means conversations with God aren't even being had anymore. I doubt the individual is still talking to God as frequently as they should. Because if they are talking to God, He will address your shortcomings. If you are not ready to address this shortcoming, then you find yourself getting farther and farther from Him. As you grow farther, your life is getting worse and worse. I am not telling you what I heard someone else say. I am telling you what I know from experience. Oftentimes, people aren't even aware of it happening until their life is in shambles. However, the book of Hebrews educates us that there is another two-edged sword that is sharper than any other two-edged swords that exist.

Hebrews 4:12, "For the word of God is quick, and powerful, and sharper than any two-edged sword, piercing even to the dividing asunder of soul and spirit, and of the joints and marrow, and is a discerner of the thoughts and intents of the heart."

Here, we learn that the word of God is a two-edged sword that is sharper than any other two-edged sword. That means that no matter what two-edged sword you encounter, the word of God can counter it. Any other sword is used to divide the soul and spirit and to cut the spirit out, causing one to get farther from God. The word of God, however, does just the opposite. It examines me and illuminates anything within my soul that is pulling me away from God. So now, instead of being led by the soul, I can be led by the spirit. If my spirit is following the Holy Spirit, then I will notice my life getting better and better.

What I love about the word of God is no matter what situation you may find yourself in, the word of God has the power to save your soul. Even if you have gotten tangled up with some strange women, or you now have a porn addiction that is difficult for you to kick, the word of God is the answer. The word of God is more powerful than anything that is coming against you. The word of God has the ability to bring you closer to Him and far out ways anything that is trying to separate you from Him. No matter what situation you find yourself in, there is an answer. The answer is the word of God, and you are never too deep into something that God cannot save you. That there is good news, and it's the gospel.

6 "For a just man falleth seven times, and riseth up again..."

Proverbs 24:16 "For a just man falleth seven times, and riseth up again: but the wicked shall fall into mischief."

This verse of scripture will really liberate an individual if they can truly grab a hold of it. The scripture starts by stating that a just man falleth seven times. On the surface, that may seem a little bit discouraging. A proverbs man's heart's desire is to be more and more like Jesus. That being said, I truly hate failing. I hate falling victim to the same tricks, and I really wish 100% of the time I could be Spirit-led. Now, with maturity, we get closer to the ultimate goal of being like Christ Jesus, but I have not yet attained this goal. I find a level of comfort in the text because it states that a just man will fall down. Now, we know that all text is inspired by God, so that means that God is more than aware of the fact that I will slip sometimes.

The next time you slip, just be reminded of the fact that God already knew this was going to happen. Don't beat yourself up for months, thinking that God looks at you differently. Way before we were even thought of by our parents, God knew everything good we would do in our lives as well as everything bad we would do. If we continue with the text, we see that a just man rises up again. The emphasis of the text is not the focus on falling but to focus on getting back up again. It reminds me of a scripture that was used in the Old Testament when they were rebuilding the temple. Solomon built a beautiful temple for the Lord, and it was destroyed by Babylon. After Babylonia captivity, God informed the people that it was time to build the temple again. God had to use Haggai the prophet to encourage the people to continue to build the temple. The people probably delayed building the temple because they figured the first temple was so major that nothing they could do with the second temple could compare to the first temple. But

God sent Haggai to tell the people the latter will be greater than the former.

The text starts with saying a just man falleth seven times, but it continues to say that the just man rises up again. I am telling you that you need to make sure that the latter part of that text is greater than the former part of the text. If you do fall, rise up so significantly that it overshadows the downfall that preceded. Thank our Lord and Savior that because of Jesus, this is a possibility. Amen.

The biblical truth that no matter how many times we fall in life getting back up is possible was a revelation I received when I was in my teenage years. I recall wanting to do better but feeling that I was too deep into trouble and that it was no way out. I felt stuck, I felt helpless, and the future seemed hopeless because the path I was on was bound to only lead to destruction. So, I did what most people do when they feel helpless—I began to weep. At that moment, God spoke. Then I finally realized that I didn't have to be stuck. My situation was not helpless. Because of Jesus Christ, I did not have to be stuck in my current situation. That revelation changed my life and had me taking a different perspective. I didn't realize it at the time, but at that moment, I began to understand the depth of His love.

In the first chapter, we discovered needing to know Him in the fellowship of His sufferings. But if we continue just one more verse, Paul says, "if by any means I might attain unto the resurrection of the dead." Paul was saying I've got to know Him in the fellowship of His suffering so I can rise from the dead myself.

One thing I love about the Bible is how brutally honest it is. Some people question whether the book is fiction or made up. If you really sit down and read it, then coming to that conclusion is impossible. If it was some fictitious book, I hardly doubt it would include the flaws of the men and women of faith. It would ignore the fact that Abraham momentarily lost sight of the promise of God and decided to birth a child outside of his marriage. It would ignore the fact that David had a man killed to cover up the fact that he was sleeping with the man's wife. It wouldn't state the previous profession of Rahab. It wouldn't inform the readers that Paul, who wrote over half of the books in the New Testament, was killing Christians before he was encountered by God on the road to Damascus. However, the Bible explains the flaws of these Bible heroes and doesn't hide their shortcomings.

The Bible lets us know that we will fall down. I know that sounds confusing, but it is inevitable. Romans 3:23 states, "For all have sinned and come short of the glory of God." However, Abraham, David, Rahab, and Paul let us know that by the grace of God, we can get back up. Because of Jesus, we no longer must stay down; we can rise from any situation that we encounter. This is encouraging for me.

Romans 1:17 "The just shall live by faith." Living by faith is walking by faith.

When you get back up and turn in the right direction, God can redeem the time. It doesn't take Him long either. I know I started reading the bible for myself probably about four years ago. I should have been reading for 10+ years, but that just wasn't my interest, if I am being honest. But when I finally started reading the Word of God diligently, it was like God put me on an accelerated program. I received so much revelation in a short period of time. I honestly don't think I could have gained more revelation if I was studying for 10+ years versus four years. I truly believe when you decide to make it right God can put you on an accelerated program where you don't miss anything, and you will end up exactly where you should have been as if you didn't mess up at all.

Psalm 23 "He restoreth my soul."

We, as human beings, are threefold beings—spirit, soul, flesh. Our soul is in a wrestling match to determine which it will follow; the spirit or the flesh. The flesh lies no good thing, and the flesh is trying to lead us to destruction. Following the flesh leads to hatred, murdering, drunkness, just to name a few; the rest can be found in Galatians 5:19-21. No one desires to have hatred in their heart, become a murder, or an alcoholic. It starts with the little things that lead to bigger things over time. It is the occasional belittling of a certain group of people that eventually leads to hatred. It is the looking down upon a certain person that minimizes their importance and thus causes you to not view them completely as a human, which can lead to murder.

When Jesus preached, He said, you have heard it said, "thou shalt not kill." But then Jesus said don't even be angry without a cause, don't even say Raca. Raca literally translates to "empty head," or basically, "you fool." By calling someone empty head, you diminish them as a human. If not addressed, this can eventually lead to murder because to you the person doesn't seem fit to live on this earth. It is the occasional drinking in social situations that can lead to becoming an alcoholic.

It is the small things that lead to big things, and that is why David wanted the Lord to restore his soul and also why we should want the Lord to restore our soul. Once our soul is restored, we are no longer led by the flesh but led by the spirit. Galatians 5:22 lets us know the fruit of the Spirit is love, joy, peace, longsuffering gentleness, goodness, faith, meekness, temperance. So, when David was asking the Lord to restore his soul, he was asking for the Lord to restore his soul to follow the spirit instead of the flesh. This would include restoring my ability to love, restoring my joy, restoring my peace, restoring my faith. If you find yourself going down a path that you know isn't good for you, just ask yourself, "Who am I being led by?" Let the Lord be your Shepherd so He can restore your soul.

He despised the shame

Hebrews 12:2 says, "Looking unto Jesus the author and finisher of our faith; who for the joy that was set before Him endured the cross, despising the shame, and is set down at the right hand of the throne of God."

I love how it says looking unto Jesus. It serves as a reminder that we are supposed to follow Him. We are also reminded that what we are going through, He went through. Therefore, we know we can follow His example of how to overcome. But the Bible says He endured the cross. Now, to break this down, we know that Jesus died on the cross, and by Him doing this, He erased all of our sins.

That includes every sin from the past, every sin in the present, and every sin in the future. By hanging on the cross, Jesus was the sacrifice for all sins that have ever been committed on earth for all people. Now, I don't want to be graphic, but I think it is necessary because when you say sin, everybody's mind goes to a different place. Most people have classifications of sins in their heads. People classify some lies as "white lies," which makes them seem so harmless and innocent. On the opposite side of the spectrum, most people also have sins that they consider to be the worst sins.

If we are being truly honest, most people have a hard time forgiving people who committed certain sins. Somehow, we tricked ourselves into thinking because we have a hard time forgiving these sins, then God must have a hard time forgiving these sins as well. We are confident that the sacrifice Jesus made on Calvary is enough for the sin I committed at 11 when I decided to lie to my teacher, but not everyone is certain that this sacrifice is sufficient for an individual who committed murder. Jesus didn't just die to pay the price for the "little" sins that have been committed, but for all of the "worst" sins that you can think of, Jesus's sacrifice is enough. Amen. And the Bible says He endured this suffering for the joy that was set before Him, and I've come to inform the readers that we are that joy. Thank you, Lord.

Then after He bore all the sins that everyone has ever committed on Himself, the verse continues to say He despised the shame and then sat down on the right hand of the throne of God. Let us talk about despising the shame first. If you look at the word despise in Greek, it is the word *kataphroneo*, which means to disdain (the feeling that something is unworthy of one's consideration) or think little or nothing of. After Jesus bore all sin on Himself, the Bible says He thought nothing of the shame. The revelation is that, even though Jesus knew He died for all sin, He wasn't the sin.

So, there was no reason to feel any shame because He knew who He was. This is very important because the verse continues to say He then sat down at the right hand of the throne of God. I know this was Jesus, and He is perfect, but think about this. If He didn't despise the shame, it could have potentially prevented Him from sitting down on the right hand of the throne of God. Again, this is Jesus, so I know He didn't struggle with this, but most humans do. To completely understand how miraculous this is, you would have to dive into the Old Testament.

In the Old Testament, it is a point of emphasis for us to understand just how holy God the Father is. One of the jobs of the priest was to make a sacrifice for other people's sins in the temple. However, the priest needed to first make a sacrifice for his own sins, or else he would not have made it back out of the temple. That is why the priest would wear something on their waist while making sacrifices. If they didn't make a sacrifice for their own sins first, they would have died in the presence of God, and someone would have had to pull them out. I am just attempting to paint a picture of just how holy and separate God the Father is. I am thankful that Jesus knew who He was. I am also thankful He didn't let the shame of carrying all the sins of the earth prevent Him from sitting down at the right hand of the throne of God where He lives forever to make intercession for us.

When you get a clear understanding of what Jesus did, then you will no longer let shame deter you from going to the throne of grace boldly. Not because of yourself but because of Jesus. Amen.

When you accept Jesus as your Lord and Savior, the Father no longer sees your sins, but He sees Jesus. If you can receive this revelation, it will revolutionize the way you see Jesus, the way you pray, and the way you view yourself. Jesus already died on the cross, so sin is no longer a problem. The problem is often the shame that is caused by the sin we committed.

We often let the shame of what we did prevent us from praying because we somehow think that God no longer hears us. I remember when I was younger, and I sinned that day, I thought I had to wait until the morning time before I could pray again. Hindsight, it sounds childish, but I was misinterpreting Lamentations 3:22-23 when it says, "his mercy is new every morning." Don't let the shame prevent you from coming back to the Lord. There is a couple of reasons why this is important. 1. If you let shame take over and make you reluctant to come back to God, then you will only get deeper and deeper in sin. 2. God already knew this was going to happen way before you were born, so this didn't catch Him by surprise. If you understand that Jesus despised the shame and then sat down at the right hand of the throne of God, then you should despise your shame and come boldly to the throne of grace.

Hebrews 4:16 says, "Let us therefore come boldly unto the throne of grace, that we may obtain mercy, and find grace to help in the time of need." The only reason we can come boldly to the throne of grace is because of Jesus.

In the verse that precedes Hebrews 12:2, it says, "lay aside every weight and sin."

This lets us know that there must be a difference between weight and sin. Maybe some of the weight we are carrying is shame from an old sin that we have yet to fully forgive ourselves of. We need to let it go so we can move forward. Thank Jesus for being a living testimony as to how we are supposed to bounce back in life. Since He already took care of the sin problem, we just need to despise the shame and come directly back to the Father. Isn't that what the prodigal son did?

The prodigal son left the presence of his father and got to a point where he was longing to eat what the pigs ate. At that moment he realized, I had it better in my father's house. Now, the Bible says he spent his money on wild living, so we know he was sinning while away from his father's house. However, at the time he was willing to eat what the pigs ate, he was no longer sinning. At that point, the only thing that could have kept him from coming back to his father's house was shame. I am simply informing you that you cannot let shame keep you from your Father. Just like the father reacted to the prodigal son returning home, the Father has the same reaction when we return to Him.

Of course, our goal is to be more and more like Jesus, who lived a sinless life. I realize only Jesus lived a sinless life, but I think my pastor said the closer we get to Him, we should be sinning less and less. I thank Jesus that He not only lived a sinless life but also was able to demonstrate how to get back up. Now I can see myself as He sees me. Sin leads to death, so I am not diminishing sin. However, we need to learn how to get back up so we don't stay in sin and can move forward, upwards, and closer to God.

This would be a good time to stop and evaluate yourself and see if any shame is potentially preventing you from coming back to God. If I could even take another step, I would evaluate what shame is keeping you from building other relationships as well. If you didn't take the time to develop a relationship with your kids for years, don't let shame prevent you from attempting to build a relationship now. If you messed up in a relationship with a spouse, don't let shame prevent you from trying to strengthen that relationship. If you fell out with your parents, siblings, friends, anyone at all, please don't let the shame of what you did prevent you from moving forward. I have seen this too many times in my life, and the person never feels good about not trying harder to build that relationship. Please don't let the shame of what you did for a season cause you to live with regrets that last for a lifetime.

Depth of His Love

Earlier in this chapter, I mentioned the depth of His love. This can be found in Ephesians 3:18. The verse mentions the width, length, depth, and height of Jesus's love. I really wish I could talk about all four dimensions of His love in the chapter, but that could probably end up being a whole other book, honestly. So, I will just briefly talk about the depth of His love.

The first component of the depth of His love can be found in Ephesians 2: 4-5, "But God, who is rich in mercy, for his great love wherewith he loved us, Even when we were dead in sins, hath quickened us together with Christ, (by grace ye are saved;)." Now, this is talking about God the Father, and Ephesians 3:18 is describing the love of Christ, but we can agree that the Father, Son, and the Holy

Spirit love the same. That means before I decided to make Jesus my Lord, God loved me. While I was yet in my sin and didn't have any desire to repent, God still loved me. The beautiful thing about this is that it means that I didn't do anything to make God love me. Which would inherently mean that I cannot do anything to make God stop loving me. His love towards me was never contingent upon my actions. We still must accept Christ as our savior to be able to fully understand just how much God loves us, but it is true that no matter what, God loves you. That right there is good news.

Another component of the depth of His love is that He loved us enough to leave heaven and come to earth. John 1:14, "For the Word was made flesh, and dwelt among us..." and the Word that the verse is describing here is none other than Jesus Christ. Now, the Bible says different things about Heaven, and we are well aware of the fact that it is the most beautiful place ever created. Matter of fact, whatever idea of heaven you have in your head, no matter how immaculate you envision heaven to be, I can assure you that it is better. Even though we are aware of how much love it must have taken to descend to earth, we may never really be able to completely understand just how much He left in Heaven until we get there. But one thing that we know for sure is that Jesus departed from the presence of the Father momentarily so that He could be with us. That is the beautiful thing about John 1:14, which explains that He dwelt among us. When He descended to earth, He didn't have to be forced to be around people; He genuinely desired to be around us because that is how much He loves us. Also, since He became flesh, that also gave Him the capability to be able to fully understand how we felt and why we struggled at times. Jesus became flesh because He truly wanted to understand us as human beings. It is one thing to say you understand what someone else is going through, but it is another thing to actually go through what someone else is going through. And He did this because He loved us.

An easily overlooked element of the depth of His love is that He chose to be from Nazareth. When Jesus came down, He was raised in Nazareth. When Philip met Jesus, he then came to Nathaniel and told him to come and see whom Moses, in the law, and the prophets wrote about. Nathaniel said to Philip, "Can any good thing come out of Nazareth." Now, if He decided to come down to earth and be raised in the influential areas, that would still be rubbish compared to heaven. However, He decided to come down to Nazareth, and to be frank, Nazareth was the hood. Not only was Nazareth the hood, but you could also tell that no one there had a high expectation of themselves. The reason I say that is because Nathaniel said can any good thing come out of Nazareth. Meaning nothing good at that point had come out of Nazareth. That's not just poverty; that is a mentality. However, Jesus saw it fit to come from Nazareth.

You know what else I love about the depth of His love? Jesus loved us so much that He went to Hell for us. Let me explain that because I am sure to a lot of people that sound like complete blasphemy. I will prove my point.

1 Peter 3:18-20 states, "For Christ also hath once suffered for sins, the just for the unjust, that he might bring us to God, being put to death in the flesh, but quickened by the Spirit. By which also he went and preached unto the spirits in prison; which sometimes were disobedient, when once the long-suffering of God waited in the days of Noah, while the ark was a preparing, wherein few, that is, eight souls were saved by water."

In there, Peter explains that Jesus preached to the spirits in prison who were disobedient in the days of Noah. When people passed away in the Old Testament, they went to Sheol (Hades), and it had two different levels. The bottom level was for people who didn't believe in God, and the top level was for individuals who did believe in God. (If you would like to verify the levels, then visit Deuteronomy 32:22 and Luke 16:19-31). Now, the spirits Jesus preached to were people who didn't believe in the Lord. So, that would mean that Jesus descended all the way to the lowest parts of Sheol. That is the reason that Jesus stated that He had the keys to hell and the grave in Revelations 1:18. By saying He had the keys, that means He went there, and He conquered it. That leads me to my conclusion regarding the depth of His love.

Jesus came to earth as a regular man, but He lived a sinless life, showing that sin doesn't have to have a stronghold on us. Jesus was born in the worst parts of Israel, but He made it out to show us that no matter where you're from, God can use you. Jesus died and descended, but He rose, and this proves He has the power of death, hell, and the grave. And I've come to tell you that because Jesus has the power of it, then that means that as long as you live in Christ Jesus, you have power over it as well. The essence of the depth of His love is it no longer matters where you're from, what you have done, what you are experiencing, there is nothing that Jesus cannot save you from. The totality of the depth of His love explained in two words is Jesus Saves!

It doesn't matter how deep you may be in sin, the same God who overcame hell can lift you up out of your situation.

Hebrews 7:25 states, "Wherefore He is able to save them to the uttermost that come unto God by Him, seeing he ever liveth to make intercession for them." In this verse, it says He ever liveth, and Revelation 1:18 states that He is alive for evermore. Amen. The uttermost means the most extreme or greatest. God is able to save us from the most extreme or greatest sins and then gives us the ability to experience His salvation to its greatest capabilities.

Saved in Greek is the word *sozo*. When people hear the word saved, they tend to think it only refers to being saved from our sins, and that is it, but it's actually deeper than that. Sozo means to save, keep safe and sound, rescue from danger or destruction, heal, to make well, restore, preserve, and of soundness of mind. While I am currently writing this, the world is at its height of the coronavirus pandemic. As I watched others react to this situation, it became apparent to me that most people don't comprehend or believe that God can save them from anything.

Not only can He protect me from it altogether, if I did end up getting sick, then the same God can heal me. Having a full understanding of the power of God would also lead one to believe that even if they became sick and passed away, the same God that can protect and heal can resurrect. This is all included in the salvation package. Another important part of salvation is that it includes a progressive and continuous process from being sinful in nature to being more and more like Jesus. Thank God for salvation. Thank God for letting me know that no matter what I encounter, no matter where I am, no matter how deep I am in sin, Jesus can save me. And because I know that Jesus saves, I can be confident that even if I fall. The same God who saves is able to help me rise up again. Amen.

Final Prayer

I thank God for revealing this to me so I can be a better man and a proverbs man. What I have learned while studying and writing this book will change my life forever. I pray that as you read this book, you are changed forever as well. I pray that something you encountered in this book motivated you, encouraged you, and provoked you to do better. I pray you keep striving towards the mark. The mark is to be more and more like Jesus. I thank God that even while you are finishing this book, God is speaking to you in a personal, intimate, and life-changing way. And from this moment forward, your life will never be the same! Amen.

About the Author

Royal Gatson is a preacher, author, supervisor, and landlord. He is passionate about helping people in various ways. He is motivated and believes all things are possible to him who believes that all things are possible. If you would like to get in contact with Royal Gatson to express how this book changed your life, please contact him at roythoughts@gmail.com

Made in the USA
Las Vegas, NV
21 May 2023